The Cloister Album of Voluntaries Volume Two

For Electronic or Pipe Organ,
American Organ, Harmonium or Piano

CONTENTS BOOK 4

© 2010 by Faber Music Ltd
This folio first published in 2001 by International Music Publications Ltd
International Music Publications Ltd is a Faber Music company
Bloomsbury House 74–77 Great Russell Street London WC1B 3DA
Managing Editor Anna Joyce
Printed in England by Caligraving Ltd
All rights reserved

ISBN10: 0-571-53472-4
EAN13: 978-0-571-53472-2

The Cloister Album
of Voluntaries Volume Two

For Electronic or Pipe Organ,
American Organ, Harmonium or Piano

CONTENTS BOOK 5

The Cloister Album
of Voluntaries Volume Two

*For Electronic or Pipe Organ,
American Organ, Harmonium or Piano*

CONTENTS BOOK 6

Andante in C
Mozart

Pastoral Symphony (from The Messiah)
Handel

Air (from Water Music)
Handel

God So Loved The World (from Crucifixion)
Stainer

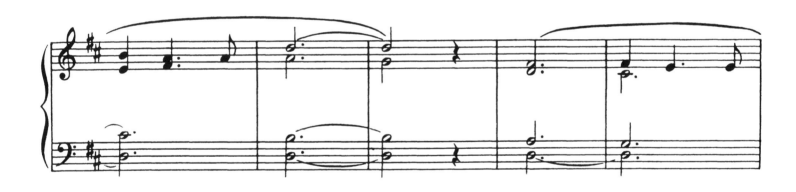

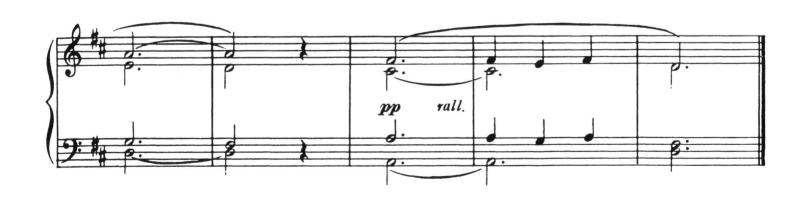

So Deep Is The Night (Tristesse)
Chopin

Ballade
Grieg

Sarabande (from Holberg Suite)

Grieg

O Rest In The Lord (from Elijah)
Mendelssohn

War March Of The Priests (from Athalie)
Mendelssohn

All Through The Night
Welsh

Poem
Fibich

Tema
Beethoven

Allegretto (from Symphony no. 7)
Beethoven

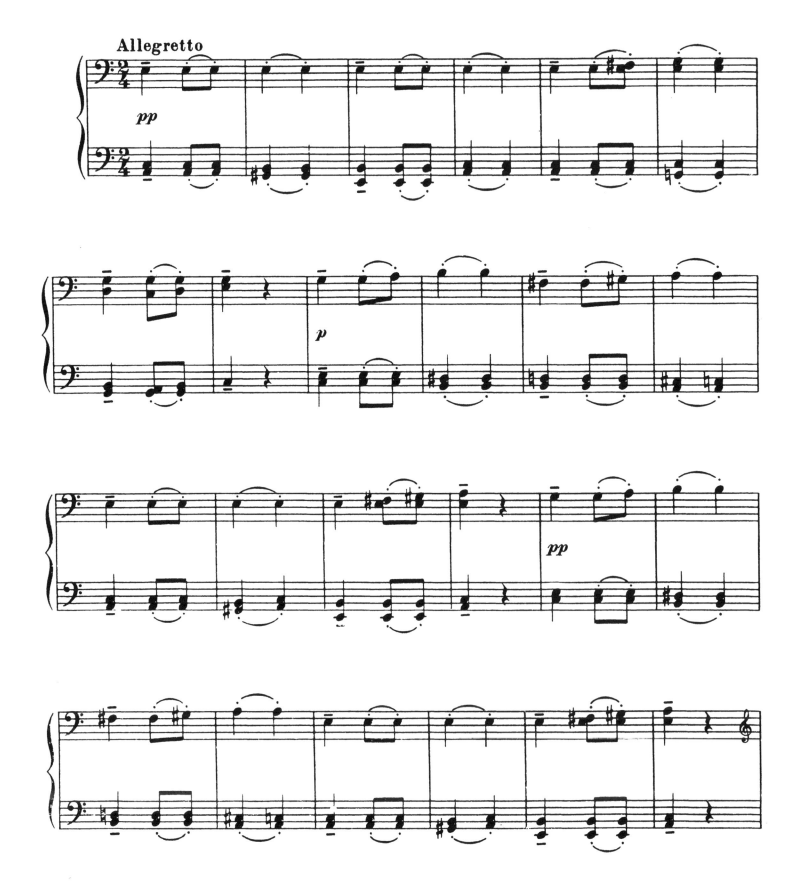

Bagatelle
Beethoven

Jesu, Joy Of My Soul (Cantata no. 147)
J.S. Bach

The Old Folks At Home
Foster

Aria (from Orfeo)
Gluck

Menuetto
Schubert

STEAL AWAY

Spiritual

Traditional

First Movement Pathétique Symphony
Tchaikowsky

MODERATO IN E MINOR

D. SCARLATTI

God Save The Queen
National Anthem

Auld Lang Syne
Scottish

Air
Anon

Allegretto (Hymn of Praise)
Mendelssohn

Allegretto un poco agitato

Andante
Beethoven

Andantino
Schubert

Chorale
Schumann

David Of The White Rock
Welsh

Deep River
Spiritual

Entry Of The Queen Of Sheba
(from Solomon)
Handel

God Is A Spirit
(from The Woman Of Samaria)
Sterndale-Bennett

Greensleeves
English

Hark! A Voice Is Calling (Wachet Auf)
J.S. Bach

Allegretto

Largo

Arne

Lullaby
Grieg

Massa's In De Cold, Cold Ground
Foster

Oft In The Stilly Night
Irish

Prelude In C

J.S. Bach

Panis Angelicus
Franck

Romance (from Eine Kleine Nachtmusik)
Mozart

Ye Banks And Braes
Scottish

Sarabande
Handel

VARIATION

Siciliano
Pleyel

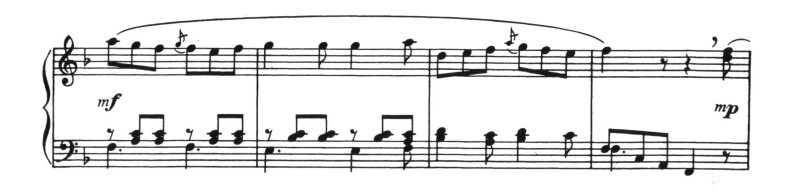

Adagio
Arne

Prelude in C minor
Chopin

Arietta

Haydn

Air
J.S. Bach

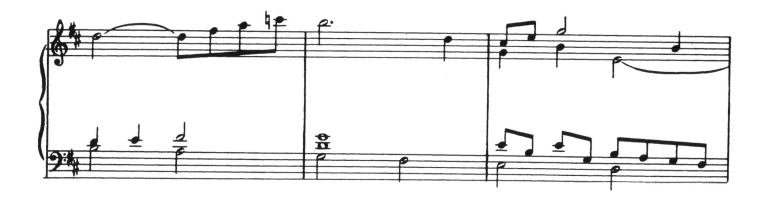

Andante Con Moto (from Symphony no. 5)
Beethoven

Believe Me,
If All Those Endearing Young Charms
Irish

Come Unto Me
Lindsay

Andante religioso

Cradle Song
Brahms

Dresden Amen (from Parsifal)

Wagner

He Giveth His Beloved Sleep

Abt

If With All Your Hearts
Mendelssohn

Drink To Me Only With Thine Eyes
Col. R Mellish

Last Spring
Grieg

Land Of My Fathers
Welsh

Loch Lomond
Scottish

Nobody Knows The Trouble I've Seen
Spiritual

Pavan (Earl of Salisbury)

Byrd

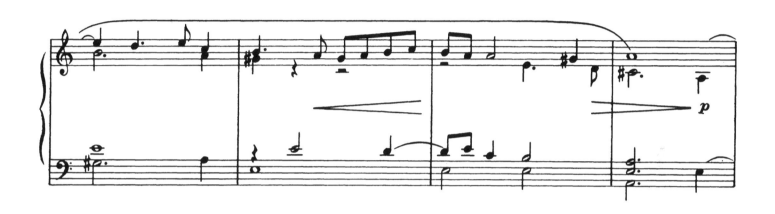

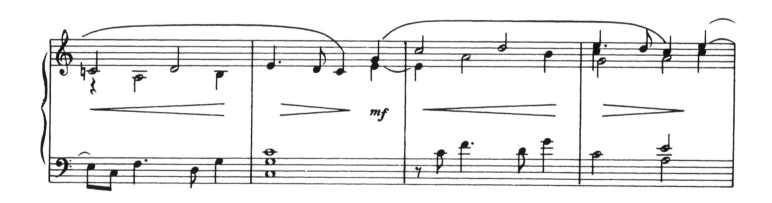

Redeem Us By Thy Grace (Cantata no. 22)
J.S. Bach

Chorale

Chorale

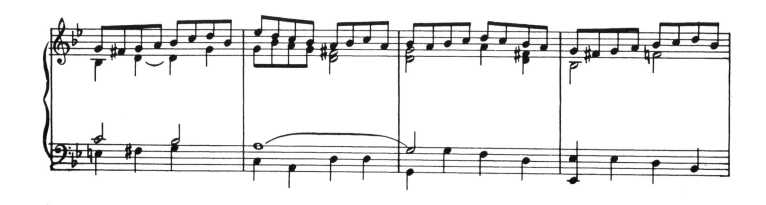

129

To A Wild Rose
MacDowell

To Music

Schubert

Until The Day Breaks
Gounod

Sarabande
Purcell

Voi Che Sapete
(from The Marriage Of Figaro)
Mozart

The Wedding (La Novia)
Prieto